The Race To Recovery

By Colleen McNamara Cimador
and Christopher G. Cimador

Illustrations by Mike Valentine

To my husband, Gerald who's love for us has no bounds. To my friends and family for their never-ending support. Thank you to my Mom for teaching me about the power of faith and nutrition. Thank you to my Father for teaching me to never give up or lose my sense of humor. And thank you to Chris for being brave enough to share his story and to Kate for being so kind and patient through it all. To the Doctors who broke the mold and started looking for answers: you are an inspiration. I thank God for being patient with me, watching over us all, and showing us the way. Thank you, all!

Contents

FORWARD BY
DR. NANCY O'HARA, MD.

To The Kids

Do you have trouble thinking in school? Has some adult told you that you have ADD or ADHD? Do you have trouble breathing, have asthma or allergies? Chris had to deal with some of these issues and wrote a book with his mom about how they found ways to make them better. He was sick of being sick, of having to use so much medicine and not having enough energy. If you are like Chris, read this book. It will help, it's fun to read and it may change your life.

To The Parents

Over the years I have learned that the most important thing you can do as a doctor or as a friend or as a person on this planet is to listen. I have learned to listen to my patients and to the moms of my patients. I have listened to them and now I ask you to listen and to learn as a parent about the amazing ways you can help your child to live a more healthy life. You can start to listen by reading this book, a wonderful story of a journey to health told in a child's voice, a funny, honest and smart young boy.

If your child has symptoms of colic or poor sleep, allergies or eczema and other rashes or a myriad of the symptoms listed at the end of this book, then please read on. If your child now has asthma, allergies, ADHD, learning problems or poor health in general, then please read on. Chris and his mom will show you in this engaging, light-hearted and well-researched book how putting the right kind of fuel into your body can help you to be healthier.

A friend of mine once said, there is no such thing as junk food, it is either junk or food. And as Chris' Mom says in the book if you "can't pronounce the ingredients, they aren't good for you." Eating a diet that is more organic, less processed and fresher, "a non-barcode diet" can help you to live a healthier life.

In addition, some of our children are sensitive to and cannot appropriately digest gluten (wheat, rye, barley and oats found in breads and cereals and pasta) and casein (dairy such as milk and cheese and ice cream). Trying to eat these foods can increase other allergies and sensitivities, hamper absorption of good nutrients and lead to allergies, eczema and even behavioral and attention problems. Removing these foods and living a cleaner life as Chris and mom describe can really help. Putting the right fuel in your car can turn it from a sputtering, stalling clunker to a sleek sports car.

It is not always easy to change your diet, to change your lifestyle, to look outside the box, but Chris and his mom did it and they weave a wonderful tale about the difference it made in their lives. This can happen for your child too. Read this book with your child, use it as an inspiration to jump start your journey to better health and enjoy. Enjoy this book, enjoy a healthier and more fulfilling life and enjoy your healthier child.

· 1 ·

How it All Began

I'm kind of your average kid. I like to run around with my friends, play sports, build stuff, and sometimes break stuff. My name is Chris.

I have a younger sister, Kate, who follows me around and sometimes drives me nuts. Don't tell her I said this, but I think she is actually pretty funny. We can have a good time together when we aren't fighting over something totally ridiculous.

Mom and Dad are pretty cool too. My Mom is really good at sports. She actually beats my Dad in basketball. He says it's because he doesn't have the right shoes on, or his old baseball injury is acting up, but I'm not sure I believe him. Dad likes to do fun stuff too. He takes me skiing, hiking and fishing, and calls me his little buddy. I usually get in trouble because my room is messy, I ask to play video games way too much and for fighting with my sister. Dad gets really mad at that last one but I'm pretty sure he fought with his sister when he was my age.

All this sounds pretty normal, but my family had to work extra hard to be your average family on the block. You see, before I became really healthy and hung out with friends and headed to basketball practice, I had a few years where

all I did was go to one doctor after the next. I had to carry around a big medicine pack and I didn't feel so healthy. My stomach hurt all the time and I would break out in hives a lot. Sometimes we didn't even know why. I was always too tired to do things other kids my age loved. Sometimes even bright lights and loud places bothered me, and I would rather just hang at home.

In the back-pack I always had to have with me there was medicine to help break down food in my stomach. I had another medicine to take for when I went outside and started to itch and sneeze. I also had one to take if I started running and couldn't breathe. My least favorite medicine was a shot I had to carry around in case I ate any of the foods I wasn't supposed to eat. It was to stop what the Doc called an ana-phylactic shock. You see pills don't work on something that serious, and with such an unpronounceable name.

I was even supposed to take medicine to help me sit still! There were many times I had to take gross pills for when I was sick and my body needed help to get better. My mom called them antibiotics but I just called them puke pills. That's what I felt like doing after I swallowed them.

It all started when I was a baby. My Grandma tells me that I was pretty adorable. I thought I looked kind of like a grem-lin, but that's my opinion. Everyone was always hugging and

kissing me, but I was always screaming and crying. I didn't sleep much either, and my head was always moving around when mom tried to feed me. It was like I was hungry but I didn't want to take the food.

Mom started to wonder if something was wrong and took me to the doctor. That's when the doctor said that my stomach needed some help breaking down my food. This was the first medicine to go in the pack. Mom wasn't really sure it worked because I just kept crying, and I still never slept. She did say that I was cute. I thought that was nice of her, considering I kept her up all night.

When I was older and tried new foods, my ears and cheeks would turn red. Mom wasn't sure what that meant,

"ALLERGENS"

but I did have nice rosy cheeks. Then came the day I got to try peanut butter. As soon as it touched my mouth my lips started to swell, and my face turned red with little bumps all over it. Mom called the doctor, and she was told to call 911 right away. The good news was that we got to ride in the ambulance and rush through all the red lights which was pretty awesome. The bad news was I felt horribly sick.

I was okay after my hospital treatment, but it turned out that I was allergic to a bunch of foods, including nuts. So the doctor gave me a shot that I could take if I ever ate any of those foods by mistake. It was the second medicine to throw in my pack.

By the time I was 5, I was sick a lot. I guess allergies took over my body. Mom told me that when you are sick there is a battle going on inside you with good guys and bad guys. It's safe to say my good guys were losing. I also couldn't breathe

in and out, especially when I tried to run fast. This made me so mad, because who wants to lose every race they run?

My friend George always pointed out how slow I was- which was not cool. Not only could I not win, I often couldn't even finish. So, off to the lung doctor we went. This doctor told us that I had something called asthma. This meant my lungs weren't working like they should. He gave me this weird looking thing called an inhaler. I had to use it if I ever felt short of breath. Kate thought it looked like a whistle. I just hoped it would help me beat George in a race one day.

So far I had medicine so I could eat and digest. I had medicine if I ate something I wasn't supposed to eat, and medicine for when I was out of breath.

I took my medicine pack, with all the instructions inside it to play dates. As mom explained how to use all my medicine, sometimes the other mom would start to scratch her head. I guess she wondered if she needed to go to nursing school just to have me over.

As I got older, it was time for me to start learning to read. I really wanted to read but sometimes my mind would wander. It was hard to focus. I also found it hard to sit still. Sometimes Mom would have to chase me around the house to get me to sit down. Kate would start to giggle, but Mom never looked too amused.

Someone told Mom that maybe there was a reason I had a hard time in school. Maybe she should take me to another doctor. So we did. This doctor said that in order for me to learn and sit still I needed to take more medicine.

After that appointment Mom sighed. "There has to be another way. We can't fit anymore medicine in this pack! I'm going to talk to some other moms and do some research."

· 2 ·

The Game Plan

I knew Mom meant business. She bought a bunch of books and went online. Sometimes I would hear her yell, "A Hah! Now THAT makes sense!" I looked at Kate and she looked at me. Kate worried that Mom was losing it. I assured her that Mom knew what she was doing. At least I hoped!

Kate asked, "Why is Mom reading so much? I thought she just read those magazines with lots of pictures of famous people. Now she reads boring books with so many words and hardly ANY pictures."

"She's trying to help me, so I can get rid of the stuff in my medicine pack."

"What?" Kate said with a look of confusion. "Mom's not a Doctor. How can she do that?"

"Pipe down, Kate! Mom is pretty serious. She looks like she's on to something. Let's just wait and see. I'm tired of carrying this thing around and feeling sick. Maybe she'll come up with a plan."

Then one day, Mom came home from the store with a

piece of paper in her hand. She looked like she was in shock. It was the same face she had when my sister was three and walked into the room after cutting her hair with scissors. She finally started to speak. "I can't believe it. Guess what I'm holding in my hand!" Given the look on her face, we were hoping it was a pass to Disneyland or some sort of winning lottery ticket. "I was at the store and look at the flyer that was right in front of my face!" The flyer said the following:

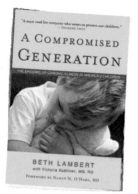

Do you have a child with:
- Food allergies?
- Autism?
- ADHD?
- Asthma?
- Gluten intolerance?
- Diabetes?
- Mood/behavioral disorders?
- Other chronic symptoms?

FIND OUT WHY AND WHAT YOU CAN DO ABOUT IT

A Compromised Generation:
The Epidemic of
Chronic Illness in
America's children

By Beth Lambert
with Victoria Kobliner, MS RD
Forward by Nancy O'Hara, MD
(Sentinent Publications, 2010)
www.acompromisedgeneration.com

Come hear Beth Lambert talk about her new
book and the epidemic at
The Darien Library 1441 Post Road
Darien CT.
Thursday, October 28th 7:00 PM

We all couldn't believe it because it was the exact thing we had been praying for lately. I asked Mom if she thought it was a direct sign from above.

"Chris, if it had been any more direct it would have hit me in the head in the form of a paper airplane made from this exact flyer and thrown by you."

We all agreed.

· 3 ·

Answers

The day of the lecture came. Mom went to hear the woman talk about why so many kids feel sick and carry around so much medicine these days. I hoped she would learn something that would help us so we waited for her to come home.

When she walked through the door, she was really excited and spoke way too fast. She told us that the woman who wrote the book had a daughter just like me who didn't feel well and also had to take a lot of medicine. Mom also said that she explained why there were so many kids getting sick in the first place.

"Mom, how does that help us though?" I asked. I mean, it's nice to know I'm not alone but did she say anything that could actually make us better?

Mom took a breath and looked at me with a smile. "Chris, her daughter is better now and doesn't need all of the medicine! She feels great which is why this awesome Mom wrote the book! She has a plan for children to get better and

feel healthier!"

Now THAT got me psyched. We finally had a game plan! Mom even had the names of a Doctor, nutritionist and suggestions for how to get started feeling better.

So the next day, Mom got on the phone and started making phone calls and scheduling my appointments.

"Chris, I've made the appointment with the doctor who was able to help the other little girl." I could tell by the twinkle in Mom's eyes that she was happy about finally finding some answers. I was glad to see her so psyched, because for a long time she had looked really worried.

Off to the doctors we went. I had my medicine pack with me just in case.

The doctor seemed nice enough, but no different than any other doctor I had met. She gave me an exam and took some blood. I didn't like that part, but she promised that a sample of my blood would give her clues about what was making me feel ill all the time. The clue part sounded kind of cool and mysterious so I went along with it and looked the other way. The rest of the check up was your average doctor visit and then we got to leave. I guess it wasn't too bad, but I still wondered what would be different about this doctor.

"I'll phone you when I have the first results of Chris's blood test. Some of the results will take a bit longer to get so we will make a second appointment when those arrive. We will discuss what can be done to make Chris feel healthier and stronger. Maybe we can start to get rid of some of that medicine. Does that sound good?"

We both thought that sounded good. We said our good-bye's but then the waiting began.

It took ten days for that phone call to happen. Who knew ten days could feel like such a l-o-n-g time! Mom and I rushed to the doctor's office. More waiting. I kept asking Mom why she kept biting her fingernails. Finally, the doctor sat us down for a chat. She looked at Mom and said, "So, your son is bothered by many of the foods he's eating."

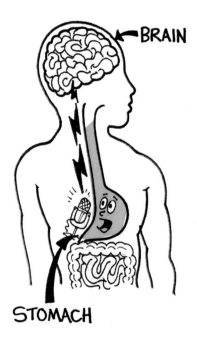

Mom said, "That's right. Chris is allergic to some foods, so he never eats them."

The Doctor smiled and said, "Yes, but there are other foods that are bothering your son's stomach and preventing it from working right. If his stomach isn't working right then his brain and body won't work right. She looked at me. "Think of your body as a car. If you don't put in the right gas, the car just won't work."

I pictured myself as a cool sports car. Although, I guess I was a broken down old sports car that didn't go very fast and had flat wheels.

That Doc taught us all sorts of things about our bodies and the food we ate. We learned that food isn't made the way it used to be made. In the old days, people used to eat their meals straight from the farm. No foods came from a box or frozen ready to eat. Fast food wasn't invented back then! I couldn't believe that there was a time when mac and cheese didn't exist.

I could hardly picture what the doctor said next. "You know Chris, lots of the food kids eat now is made in labs and in factories.

I pictured people in white scientist coats, beakers every-where, creating food concoctions. She explained further. "Artificial dyes and preservatives are added to the food so they last longer on the grocery store shelf, and to make them look brighter and more appealing."

She also said that many fruit and vegetable seeds are made in a lab before being planted. This just keeps getting weirder and weirder I thought to myself.

She continued. "It turns out, these days many farmers spray with lots of pesticides as their crops grow. Pesticides are used to kill bugs and stop diseases from attacking the seeds and crops. Even the animals are fed antibiotics that are hard for our bodies to break down."

Doc added that all these chemicals can make us sick and

our minds not work well. This, along with more pollution in the environment, could be why there are so many children like me that become ill and have to take so much medication.

My mind was spinning. I guess I never thought about where my food came from, I just cared about how it tasted. Now I'm finding out that a lot of what I eat is tainted with chemicals. Even the animals we eat are taking puke pills! Way gross.

Mom's eyes grew wider and wider as she listened to the doctor. She finally blinked and then asked, "If we eat food without the chemicals, would it be possible to get rid of some of the medicine in Chris' pack?

We watched the doctor closely. It was as if her mouth was moving in slow motion. We couldn't wait for the answer.

"Y - E - S! "The good news is that more and more stores are selling foods without chemicals. You can buy snacks and treats without fake dyes and preservatives, and meat and fish that are raised the old fashioned way. If you see the word organic, it means they didn't spray chemicals on the fruits and veggies. The best food for you to eat is the food you cook at home in your kitchen. The Doc grinned at me. There are tons of cookbooks to choose from that have yummy recipes to try.

Mom and I thanked the Doctor for all of the information she was giving us. She let us know that the last results from my blood test would be available in a couple of weeks. We would then meet with her again to go over them. For now, Mom and I were happy that there was a chance to feel better and get rid of the medicine.

· 4 ·

Let's Get to Work

"**D**o you think this will work, Mom.?" I asked.
"Chris, all of the research I have done told me that
this is the best chance we have to heal your body and get you
off medicine. There are lots of children eating this way to
feel better all over the country. I really think this could work
and our whole family will be healthier!"

When we got home, we told Dad and Kate all about the
appointment and what we had learned about food. Kate still
couldn't believe that there were chemicals on her broccoli.
"I ate broccoli because you said it was good for me and now
I find out it has bad stuff on it? At least I don't have to eat it
anymore!"

Mom grinned and said. "You still need to eat your broccoli, Kate. It IS good for you. We just need to buy meat, fruit
and veggies that are labeled ORGANIC, that's all."

We went to work right away and threw out everything in
our house with chemicals in it. We started with the stuff Mom
used to clean the house. Mom learned that these things

can really hurt your body and make my asthma worse. Kate was worried that our house would get really dirty and smell like my gym socks. Mom told her that we must buy natural cleaners, and they will smell even better than the chemical cleaners!

Next we threw out all the food that had ingredients Kate and I couldn't pronounce. Mom said if you can't pronounce the ingredients they probably aren't healthy.

Then came the stuff that contained food dye. Some products contain natural coloring but many other's use chemicals. We learned that the chemical food dye is actually made

out of petroleum. At first I didn't know what that meant but I found out that petroleum is oil. Yuck! I've been eating oil?

Then I remembered the doctor saying you need to put the right gas into a car for it to work right. So I thought to myself. "I'm a human not a car, I can't run on oil and chemicals!" I'm pretty sure I need food to work right. Something seems totally weird about all of this, so I kept trashing everything we found with chemicals.

We went shopping and bought all sorts of new and healthy food to eat. I was happy to see there were still yummy treats I could have!

The first few days were sometimes fun and sometimes hard. Mom let me pick out a lot of stuff at the food store which was cool. Sometimes I asked for snacks that I used to eat but couldn't anymore. This made me kind of mad, but Mom always found something similar for me to try. Then I realized that almost every unhealthy food had a healthy choice you could eat instead. I also noticed that my stomach hurt a lot less and I had tons of energy which was pretty awesome.

· 5 ·

What in the World is Gluten?

Mom was cooking one of the new recipes she discovered when she got a phone call. She said. "It's the doctor. The rest of your blood tests results are in."

So off we went to the doctor to hear what the latest clues from my blood showed. I was a little nervous. I hoped she found something that could help me become healthier.

When we arrived, Mom was excited to let the doctor know all of the changes we had made and the great food we had bought. The doctor told Mom that we had done a wonderful job at getting started!

She then turned to me and said, "Chris, your blood test has shown that eating gluten isn't good for your body. It has been really hurting your stomach and affecting how everything works inside of you. Until your stomach is healed, you should also hold off on dairy. It can be very hard to digest. You need to eat foods that are good for your stomach and can heal it."

I wasn't sure what this meant or even what gluten was but the Doc explained.

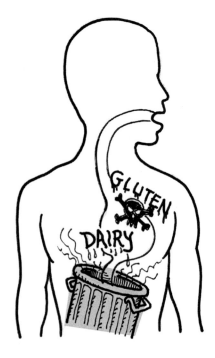

"Gluten is a protein that is used in lots of foods like bread, cereals and even the glue used on an envelope! It's grown very differently now than when your mom and I were young. It is also sprayed with harmful chemicals that can be damaging. It's changed so much that sometimes our bodies aren't sure what to do with it. Your body doesn't make the things that are needed to break it down, and if you can't break down the gluten, your stomach won't work right. You won't be able to absorb vitamins and nutrients from the food you eat.

"Wait a minute, did she just say I can't eat things like bread and cereal? Uh oh! why do I get the feeling that cookies and pizza are included in this food group? UGH!"

The Doc kept talking to Mom, but all I saw was her mouth move. I was thinking about the pizza party at school coming up on Friday. What about my birthday cake next month? I started to freak out.

Then I remembered she had also said something about dairy.

"Did she say dairy too? Maybe I heard that wrong. Please tell me I heard that wrong. Then two words screamed to me in my head. I C E C R E A M !!!!! What about this summer at the beach? What about the ice cream truck?

Mom looked over at me and saw my face. I thought I was hiding my freak out session pretty well but Mom could see right through it.

"Chris, did you hear the doctor sweetheart? Did you understand what she was saying?"

If she only knew about the conversation I just had with myself. It wasn't pretty.

"Yes, Mom. She told me that I can never eat pizza, birthday cake or ice cream again."

The doctor turned to me with a look on her face that told me this wasn't the first time she had heard a kid say this to her.

"Chris, I know that this sounds really hard and upsetting at first. Believe it or not, I know how you feel. You see, the reason I know all about this way of healing children is because I had to heal my own son this way too."

I stopped and looked up at her. She had grabbed my attention. You know when you see your teacher at the grocery store and you think it's totally weird, because you always picture them living and sleeping at school and never doing anything else? That's what I felt about my doctor. She had a son? He had a big medicine pack too?

She showed me a picture of her son when he wasn't feeling so well. He was pale with dark circles under his eyes and

didn't look too happy. I have to admit, he kinda looked like me. Then she showed me a picture of him now. He looked all healthy and sporty.

Even though I was feeling pretty mad and upset, looking at that picture and knowing the doctor had to go through this with her son, made me feel better. I would at least listen.

Then she gave us the answer that we had been wondering about for so long. She actually had an answer for why my medicine pack was so full.

"Remember when I told you last time about all the chemicals and food dyes affecting your stomach? Well, the gluten does the same thing. It can make you feel pretty sick when you can't break down food the right way. There are lots of messages and signals meant for your brain that are first made in your stomach. If your stomach isn't working your body can't make and send the right messages. So things like learning to read and sitting still in school can be extra hard." She said that even my asthma and food allergies could be made worse by all of the things I was eating that were wrong for my body.

I thought about everything she was telling me. If I wasn't taking in any vitamins maybe that's why I was always tired and George always beat me. I thought of me as a sports car again. It sounded like the gas I was getting wasn't right for the car and the gas I DID get never made it to the engine. It was all starting to make sense.

She warned us that it wouldn't be easy at first but she promised we would get used to eating a new way. It will just become normal.

At first I worried about all the things I could no longer eat. I was sad and glad all at the same time; if that's even possible. Then I started to think what my life could be if it worked.

Could I run fast without having to stop and take medicine? Maybe I could even beat George, or be a star on the school basketball team. Could I be one of the best readers in my class?

Maybe I could sit all day in class and get straight A's. And most of all maybe I could finally get rid of all of the medicine in my pack! I thought about all of the awesome possibilities.

I guess the doctor could tell by the look on my face what was going through my mind. "Chris, how do you feel about everything that I'm telling you?"

"Well, I'm kind of sad about not being able to eat certain things but happy you found out what was wrong with my body. If eating this way can make me feel better and get rid of my medicine pack, then it's worth it. It looks like it worked for your son, so maybe it will work for me too.

"Good for you Chris." She smiled and ruffled my hair. "Being willing to try is more than half the battle, kiddo. I can also promise you it's not just my son that it worked for. I see so many children that must eat this way to feel better. You are not alone."

She turned to Mom. "Your son is going to be fine. I see how strong and brave he is. I'm sure he will be brave about these changes as well. I'm just a phone call away if you need me!"

She turned to me and held up her hand for a high five. "Keep up the good work, Buddy." So off we went with my new plan of action.

· 6 ·

Did it Work?

Slowly but surely I felt myself running faster without having to stop. In school it was easier to sit still and listen. My mind calmed down and let me focus more on what the teacher was saying. I even started reading book after book! My stomach felt better and my body became stronger. Grandma even said I had a healthy glow. I'm not sure what that meant, but I guess it was a compliment.

It turns out that the pizza place around the corner from us delivers gluten free pizza with a special dairy free cheese I can eat. Mom also found a few bakeries that make allergy friendly birthday cakes and treats. I can also eat sorbet, fruit pops and fudge bars as my ice cream. Mom keeps finding more and more places that have allergy friendly menus and options. So it wasn't the end of the world when I was told my new game plan of eating. Of course these are mostly treats I'm talking about, but Mom cooks awesome healthy food all the time, so I can have these things too once in a while!

Finally, the day I had waited for so long arrived. Guess

who challenged me for another race? That's right, George! George didn't know all I had been doing to get healthier and stronger, and I wasn't about to tell him until AFTER the race. The class stood by to watch what was usually a predictable ending. Kate covered her eyes and could barely watch. I yelled, "On your mark, get set- GO!

I ran faster than I ever thought I could. At first we were tied, then something happened. Where I used to have to

stop and rest, I had a burst of energy and my legs went faster
and faster. My body didn't want to slow down. It was like I
felt lighter and all of my sickness and medicine was dropping
behind me until I was free of it. I didn't stop until the finish
line. As I looked back, George was bent over and the class

was stunned. I DID IT! I beat George! Everyone wanted to know what had happened to me, especially George. After my big win, I figured it was only fair to let them in on the secret.

· 7 ·

Spreading the News

After a time we were able to sit down and sort through my medicine pack. We threw away the medicines I no longer needed. One by one, the pack became lighter. We lost touch with all the doctors I used to know so well. Instead of check-ups and tests, I had basketball and sleepovers with friends.

One day Mom came to me and said, "Because you were brave and tried this new way of living, maybe we can help other children empty their medicine packs too."

I let Mom know what happened on the playground with George, and how I told all of my friends how I got healthier. I guess I was already helping a little, but maybe there was a way to tell more people. That's when we came up with the idea about this book. Mom and I also started a web site that tells you all about how to be healthier. I came up with some of the designs, it was actually pretty cool seeing it all come together.

You know, there were times that were hard – even when I had a plan to follow. But the hardest times were way earlier, when I felt sick and didn't know why. I hope if you're reading this book, you will try some of the things I did to become healthy and strong. Maybe you have a bunch of medicine you want to get rid of too! Give it a try. The worst that can happen is your whole family ends up really healthy.

Oh, and in case you were wondering, George and I joined the track team and we still race one another. Let's just say George is working really hard to win back his title. I even got straight A's on my report card. Now my teacher wants to know what happened too!

Check out the info my Mom and I put together on the last page of the book. We tell you how to start getting healthy

and feeling better! If you have questions for us, just log onto our web site and we would love to chat with you!

www.thedishonhealing.com

www.facebook.com/thedishonhealing

@Dishonhealing

Dishonhealing@gmail.com

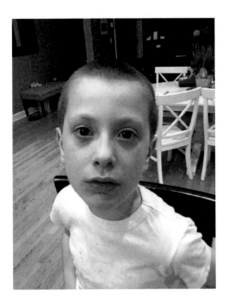 

Please send your accounts of recovery to dishonhealing@gmail.com and let's have our next book be filled with YOUR stories of recovery!

THE ROADMAP TO RECOVERY

For The Parents

If your child has been given a diagnosis and you aren't sure where to start, we've been there! The main reason we wrote this book was to give families a roadmap of where to begin their journey. We have laid out the steps that will take you on the road to recovery.

The first step is to research and fully understand the diagnosis. Once this has been done, you need to ask yourself if you are open to learning about alternative treatments. Many times the child is simply prescribed medicine or school services to address the problem. Often there is an underlying biological health issue that needs to be addressed in order for the symptoms that are present to dissipate. If your child's body isn't functioning properly symptoms may include the following:

· Autism
· Sensory/Auditory Processing Disorder

- Colic
- Asthma
- Diabetes
- Food Allergies
- Learning Disabilities/Dyslexia
- ADHD
- GI Issues
- Skin rashes
- Low muscle tone
- Poor Sleep
- Socialization Issues

The second step on the road to recovery is ridding your child's environment and diet of toxins. The following resources can guide you on this exercise.

Epidemic Answers:
www.epidemicanswers.org
The Dish On Healing (Our blog detailing our recovery):
www.thedishonhealing.com
The Feingold Diet:
www.feingold.org
Environmental Working Group:
www.EWG.org

Generation Rescue:

www.generationrescue.org

The final step should be to seek out a medical professional who can assist you in addressing any underlying medical issues that may be affecting your child's health and producing their symptoms. The following links can help you find an integrated medical doctor in your area and assist you in getting started with your new health plan.

The Medical Academy of Pediatric Special Needs:

www.medmaps.org

Talk About Curing Autism:

www.tacanow.org

THE DISH ON HEALING'S
RESOURCE LIBRARY

A Compromised Generation, by Beth Lambert

Achieving Victory Over A Toxic World, by Mark Schauss, MBA, DB

Healthy Child Healthy World, by Christopher Gavigan

The Body Ecology Diet, by Donna Gates

Gut and Psychology Syndrome: Natural Treatment for Autism, ADD/ADHD, Dyslexia, Dyspraxia, Depression, Schizophrenia, by Natasha Campbell-McBride

Outsmarting Autism, by Patty Lemur

Almost Autism, by Maria Rickert Hong

The Hidden Connection, by Kathleen DiChiaria

I Know You're In There, by Marcia Hinds

Healing Without Hurting, by Jennifer Giustra Kozek

All Natural Mom's Guide To The Feingold Diet, by Sheri Davis

DOCUMENTING **HOPE**

Chris and I would love for you to support or simply learn more about The Documenting Hope Project! Have your parents log onto **www.documentinghope.com** and watch the trailer.

You can see more kids like Chris who were feeling sick and yet recovered the same way he did. This project will track 14 other children's stories of recovery. There will also be a scientific study done to prove once and for all that kids can...RECOVER!

We can no longer accept the following statistics as the new norm:

· Autism: 1 in 50
· ADD/ADHD: 1 in 10
· Asthma: 1 in 8
· Allergies: 1 in 3
· Obesity: 1 in 3
· Learning Disabled: 1 in 6

Please support
Documenting Hope
and change the course
of these children's lives
and possibly an entire
generation!

About the Authors

Colleen McNamara Cimador is a mother of two and currently enrolled at the Institute of Integrated Nutrition to become a Holistic Health Coach. She is the author of **www.thedishonhealing.com** blog that provides a roadmap to healing many chronic illnesses with functional medicine and nutrition. During her high school years, Colleen was voted "class clown." She then went on to become a college athlete and was voted into the Hall of Fame for basketball at the University of Delaware. During her professional career, Colleen worked in online sports advertising sales in New York City until Christopher was born. She is the first to say her most rewarding title is that of a mother.

Christopher Cimador is an active 9-year-old boy who loves to draw, play basketball, ski, and hang with his friends. In his short life, he has had quite a health journey and hopes his experience can help others. He makes his family laugh each day and lives life to the fullest.

Made in the USA
Middletown, DE
30 April 2015